Is This Your First Funeral?

A Child's Primer

Jimmy Huston

Copyright © 2018 Jimmy Huston

ISBN: 978-1-970022-34-6

All rights reserved, including the right to use or reproduce this book or portions thereof in any form whatsoever without written permission from the publisher except in the case of brief quotations embodied in critical articles or reviews.

All images are used under license from Shutterstock.com

Cosworth Publishing
21545 Yucatan Avenue
Woodland Hills CA 91364
www.cosworthpublishing.com

For information regarding permission,
please send an email to office@cosworthpublishing.com.

*Dedicated to
grandma and grandpa
and gramma and gramps.*

This is a sad time.

You've heard you're going to a funeral.

You may be wondering what that means.

This is a guide to some of the things you may experience along the way.

The word is death. There's no getting around it.

It's the reason you're reading this book.

Loss

Someone is gone from your life.

A funeral is everyone's chance to say good-bye. It's a way to share the moment.

It's a moment of respect.

If you've never lost someone like this before, it's an especially hard time.

Sometimes a person's death is not a surprise, because of age or health.

That's bad enough. Sometimes it's a tragic surprise, an accident, a sudden health issue, a crime, or even an act of war.

It can be even more shocking when it's someone young. A teenager, a child, or an infant. It's not fair, but it happens.

What's a funeral going to be like?

What do I have to do?

Is it going to be scary?

How am I going to feel?

Don't worry. Everything is going to be fine.

If you're really worried about going to this funeral, here's a thought. Maybe you don't have to go.

Explain how you feel to an adult that you can confide in. Explain why you don't want to go. Perhaps you won't have to.

Feelings

When someone is lost, it hurts.

Time helps a little, but it's slow.

A lot of thoughts will come rushing in. Sad thoughts, sure, but also happy thoughts. Even funny thoughts.

You are stronger than you feel.

Condolences

That's giving and receiving sympathy. And empathy, which is a heartfelt word for sharing.

It's how we help each other get through sad times.

Crying

It's okay to cry. And, it's okay not to cry. Everyone faces things in their own way.

Laughing

It may seem strange and out of place, but you're going to see people laughing. How is that possible?

It may be a release, a letting go of feelings.

It may be a celebration of the person who's gone, or a memory of better times that were shared.

Hugging

There will be a lot of hugging (whether you like it or not). Try to understand the feelings involved. Hugs can help us all.

Sharing

Your thoughts are important to others.

You're not just sharing stories and memories.
You're sharing laughs and you're sharing pain.

Your feelings help other people, and theirs can help you.

Anger

When people die unexpectedly, a lot of emotions are left behind. One of the most surprising is anger — anger at the person who died.

That hardly seems fair at first, but it's normal. There is often unfinished business — or emotional ties that will never have a chance to be finished or resolved. It feels like a betrayal. It's okay to feel this way.

Arguing

When things get tense or emotional, people relieve the strain in unusual ways. Sometimes they argue. It can seem like two or more people who usually get along will never see peace again.

Travel

It's not unusual to travel for a funeral. It could be a short car ride, but it could also be a long trip, perhaps even across the country.

The mood of the trip can be completely different than the reason for it. Everybody else thinks it's a normal day. They don't know why you're traveling.

The Funeral Home

You will probably go to a funeral home where they take care of all of the arrangements.

This is where the departed is kept until the funeral. Sometimes people go there to view the person and say farewell.

It's normal to be curious, but it's also okay if you don't want to go.

Flowers

There will be lots of flowers everywhere. Maybe even too many flowers.

Flowers mean different things to different people. They bring back memories. They symbolize hope.

Enjoy them.

Religion

Many people take comfort in religion, especially in difficult times like this. A priest, minister, imam, or rabbi can offer guidance in difficult times.

Depending on the faith of the person, you may learn about a different religion than your own.

Ceremonies

Most funerals take place in either a place of worship or a funeral home.

People will speak about the departed. There may be a short sermon, along with prayers and songs. Some services are formal and hushed. Others are friendly and loud, with lots of stories and laughter amid the sadness.

Often, the person is there, lying in a casket. It may even be open so that people can say good-bye. You may want to see the person for one last time, but you don't have to. Sometimes the casket is already closed.

There will be lots of memories to share. There may be photographs of the person's life. There might also be home movies or videos. Or music that was important to him or her.

Speaking Up

People will be talking about the departed.

It will happen during the ceremony, and at any memorial service, but it will also happen more than that.

It may be a speech in front of a room full of listeners, but it also may be more casual than that, like comments over a meal or while riding in a car.

Grownups will be doing most of the talking, but when a kid wants to say something, they are often allowed, and even encouraged, to speak.

Kids sometimes say things more clearly and eloquently than adults. You may want to tell a story, or you can just say what the person meant to you.

If you think you will want to express your thoughts, let someone know. You may be surprised by how pleased they are to hear from you.

Just speak from your heart.

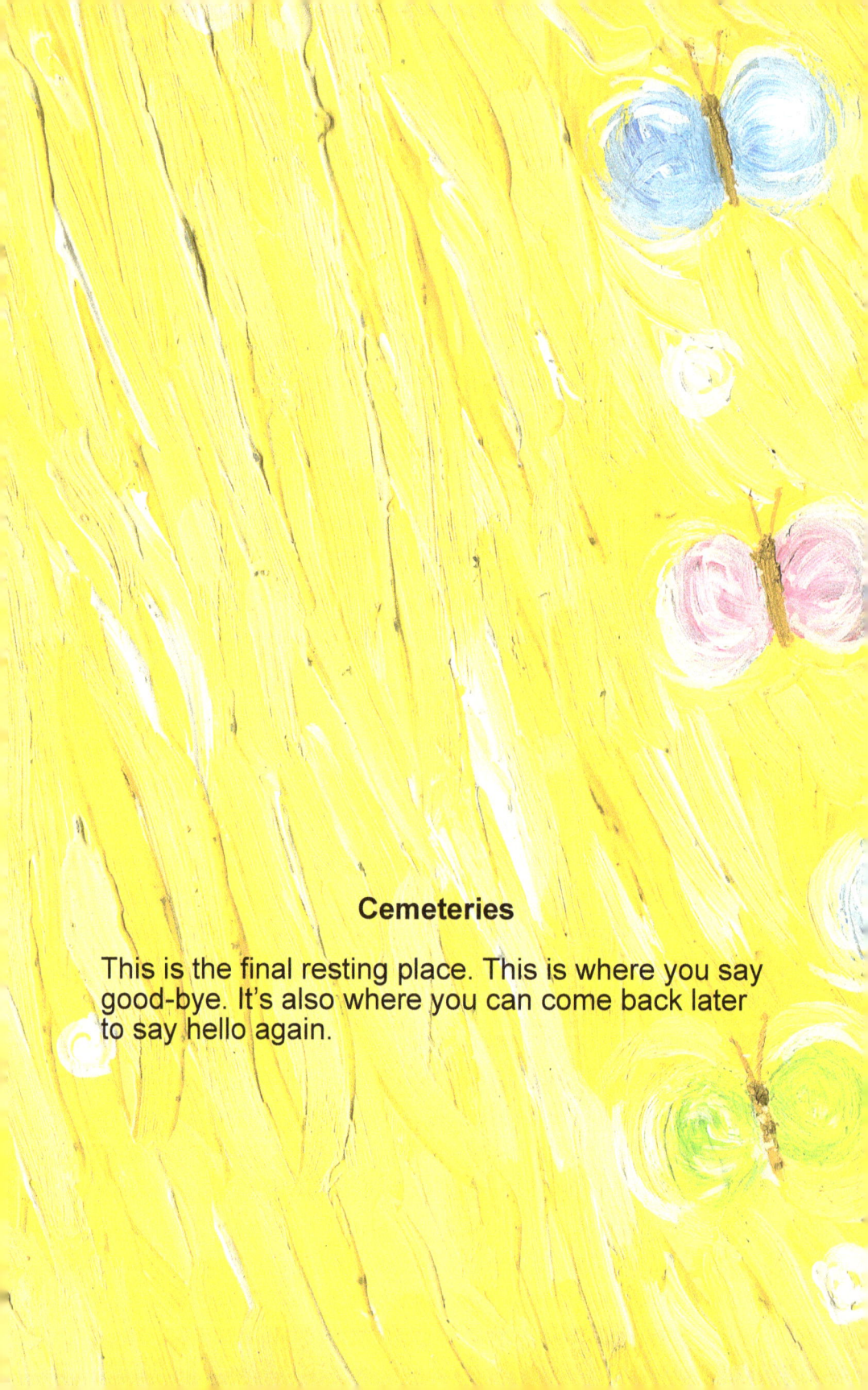

Cemeteries

This is the final resting place. This is where you say good-bye. It's also where you can come back later to say hello again.

Burial

It's a strange thing to watch someone be lowered into a hole in the ground and then be covered up with dirt and flowers. Then, it's over.

After that, everything is about healing and going forward. People will probably get together somewhere and talk and eat and drink. It slowly starts to get better.

Cremation

Some families choose cremation instead of burial. The remains are burned until they are converted into ash. This is an ancient tradition in many cultures.

Afterwards, the ashes are usually spread in a special place with a few close friends and family members attending. It could be at the seaside or on a mountaintop or some other special place.

Grief

After the loss of a loved one, grieving can get kind of crazy. It can be anything. It's the way someone deals with the loss, the tragedy, the sense of abandonment.

It can be as simple as crying, but it can go big.

Grieving can last a long, long time — and that's okay. It's how we heal.

Celebration

Strangely enough, part of grieving is celebrating. Every life deserves a celebration. You can call it a wake or a party. There will probably be even more stories, some songs, a few bad jokes, and perhaps some drinking. And lots of good food!

Memorial

Any special way of remembering can be a memorial.

Memorials can take many forms. It may be a graveside monument or a special donation to a charity. A memorial can be online, or it can be a work of art or a park.

It could also be another party or celebration that is removed from the sadness and mourning of most funeral services.

Memorials can be services that take place at a lake or a beach or a restaurant or wherever people can gather and celebrate.

Remembering

Long after the funeral and the memorial service, you'll still have thoughts about all this and about all the good times that came before it.

People in some faiths believe that a person is alive as long as that person is remembered by others, and that's a nice thought.

Know that you'll have memories of this person for the rest of your life.

And when it's all over, a funeral is also a way to remind ourselves how good it is to be alive.

Glossary

You probably know most of these words, but you may hear new words, or words used in a new way.

beloved - sometimes used to mean the dead person.
benediction - the closing prayer of a ceremony.
bereaved - the loved ones left behind.
casket - a burial container for remains.
coffin - another word for casket.
condolences - an expression of sorrow to another.
coroner - a doctor who examines the body.
cortege - a funeral procession.
cremation - converting a body to ashes.
death - the end of a person's life.
deceased - a person who has died.
departed - the person who has "left."
empathy - sharing feelings with another.
funeral - a ceremony at the end of one's life.
funeral home - a place for viewing and mourning.
hearse - a dignified vehicle for transporting remains.
interment - placing a body in a grave or tomb.
memorial - any form of remembering.
monument - a headstone for a grave.
mortuary - where funeral arrangements are made.
mourning - sharing feelings for the loss of a life.
procession - the group of cars going to a cemetery.
remains - a person's body after death.
shiva - a seven day mourning period.
sympathy - an expression of shared grief.
urn - a vessel for storing ashes after cremation.
vigil - a shared watch after a death.
wake - a celebration of life after a funeral.

About the Author

Jimmy Huston is a native of Athens, Georgia, but now lives in Woodland Hills, California with his wife and dog. He is a sometime screenwriter and filmmaker. His hobbies are complaining and not dancing.

Other odd children's books from Jimmy Huston
www.byjimmyhuston.com

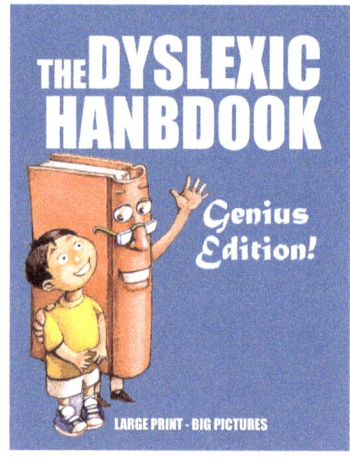

More books from Jimmy Huston
www.cosworthpublishing.com

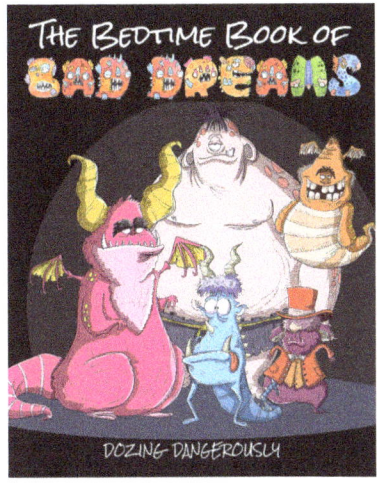

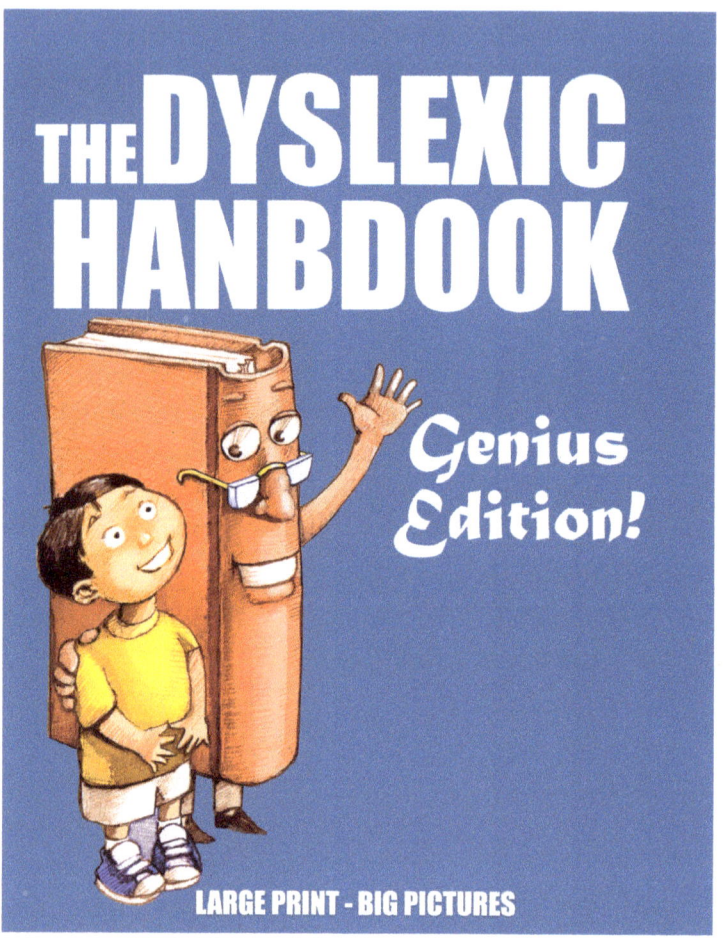

Who* buys a book for a kid with dyslexia?

Giving a self-help book to a dyslexic kid is like offering a drink of water to someone who is drowning.

So, have someone read it to you, so you can listen and think about it — and look at the pictures.

This book is also available on Audible as an audiobook. (You'll have to imagine the pictures.)

* Someone who cares.

Other books from Cosworth Publishing
www.cosworthpublishing.com

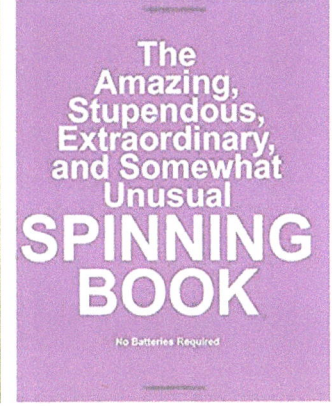

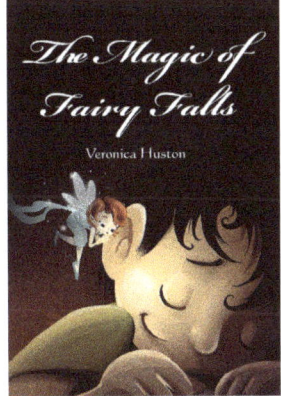

Find it wherever good books are dreaded.

If you're reading this, you will not like this book. It's not for you.

This book is for all the people who are *not* reading this.

They won't like it either, but it's short.

They'll like that.

"I didn't actually read this book. If I had, I would have loved it — but I never will." Billy

"Hate isn't a strong enough word for me. I loathe reading. I don't even like looking at pictures - which there are none of." Wally

"This isn't what I wrote about this stupid book."

Zane

"This is an excellent coffee table book, if your coffee table hates to read." Solomon

"This book made my teacher cry."

David

"My son loved this book. He said it was delicious."

Mr. Jones

"THIS BOOK IS SO DUMB THAT I COULD'VE WRITTEN IT." Jimmy

www.i-hate-to-read.com

Other books from Cosworth Publishing
www.cosworthpublishing.com

Helpful Titles from Cosworth Publishing
www.cosworthpublishing.com

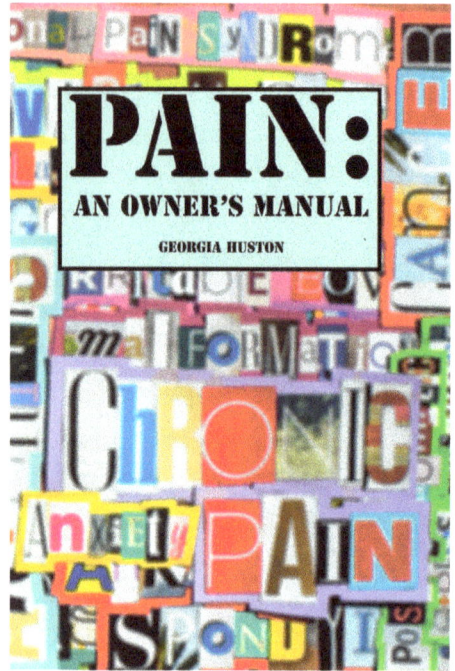

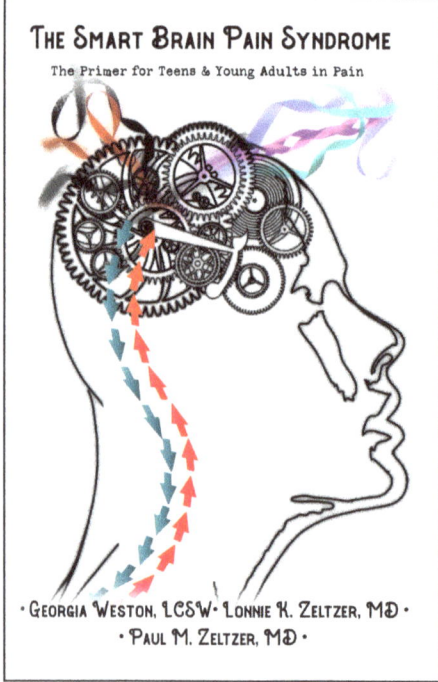

Thanks for buying, borrowing, or swiping this wonderful book.

At Cosworth Publishing we truly appreciate that, and in return, we'd like to offer you one of our E-books absolutely free—and worth every penny.

Just let us know that you want it, and we'll make sure that you get it. Let us know which book you read so we don't send you the same one.

Send an email to *office@cosworthpublishing.com*.

Then, from time to time, we will let you know via email when we have a new book that you might be interested in.

We won't do that very often because we're basically pretty lazy, and we don't produce very many new books.

Reviews are greatly appreciated.

www.ingramcontent.com/pod-product-compliance
Lightning Source LLC
Chambersburg PA
CBHW040250090526
44586CB00040B/2727